✠

COPTIC ORTHODOX
PATRIARCHATE

See of St. Mark

RETURN TO GOD

BY
H. H. POPE SHENOUDA III

Title   :Return to God
Author   :H. H. Pope Shenouda III.
Translated by :Mrs. Glynis Younan
Press   :Dar El Tebaa El Kawmia.
Edition   :August 1989 - Ist edition.
Legal deposit :No.:5607 /1989
Revised   :COEPA 1997

H.H. Pope Shenouda III
117th Pope and Patriarch of Alexandria
and the See of St Mark

CONTENTS

INTRODUCTION

CHAPTER 1 SIN IS BEING SEPARATED FROM GOD

Sin is the state of being separated from God and His saints

Sin is being cut off from the community of saints

The serious consequences of being cut off from God and the possibility of returning to Him.

CHAPTER 2 THE RETURN TO GOD

The story of man's separation from God.

What does it mean to return to God?

God wants us to return

Prayer is the means of returning

Adversity as a reason for returning to God

CHAPTER 3 RECONCILIATION WITH GOD

Sin is contending against God

Sin is being unfaithful to God

God is reconciled with us

How reconciliation takes place

In The Name Of The Father,
The Son And The Holy Spirit.
One God. Amen.

As long as sin is a state of being separated from God, then repentance will be the means of returning to God.

As long as sin is being opposed to God, or being unfaithful to Him, then repentance will be the means of reconciliation with God.

This book deals with these two subjects.

INTRODUCTION

The first part of this book deals with two themes:

1 Sin is being cut off from God:

I gave two lectures on this subject in the Cathedral at Cairo in October 1976 and July 1979.

2 The return to God:

The three lectures which I gave on this theme, in the Cathedral, were entitled, 'Return to me and 1 will return to you' (August 1977), 'The return to God' (June 1980) and 'Returning to God' (July 1981).

The second part is about 'Reconciliation with God'

This is based on lectures which I gave in March 1975 and November 1976 in the Cathedral, along with two others, entitled, 'How can I be reconciled with God', given in November and December 1970. In addition to these is another lecture entitled, 'Sin is disloyalty', which was given during Holy Week in 1973.

This book is the fruit of these ten lectures.

Shenouda III

✥

CHAPTER 1

SIN IS BEING SEPARATED
FROM GOD

Sin Is The State Of Being Separated From God And His Saints

What is the spiritual life? Is it not being close to God, as the the Psalm says "*But it is good for me to draw near to God.*" *(Ps. 73:28).*

It is indeed! it is however, something more than this closeness. It means to abide in the Lord, according to what He told us: "*Abide in Me, and I in you.*" *(John 15:4).*

A person whose life is firmly established in the Lord, enjoys His companionship and His love. He keeps God in his heart, while he himself dwells in God's heart.

Is a sinner someone who abides in God, who remains steady in His love? No, not at all! **The sinner follows another path, not God's path.**

The sinner has cut himself off from God through his behaviour, his manner and his will. His will has become something other than God's will. He begins to want what God does not want. He becomes a person who challenges God fearlessly and breaks His commandments. In breaking God's commandments, he will have also cut himself off from God's love, because the Lord says: "*If you keep My commandments, you will abide in*

My love." (John 15:10) and, *"If anyone loves Me, he will keep My word." (John 14:23).*

Therefore, sin is the state of being separated from God's love and from His commandments. It is the life of a person who has renounced God and His kingdom in order to be independent and who has begun to follow his own desires without putting God before him.

Such a person has become cut off from God and persists in the belief that he has an independent personality which can stand on its own and determine whatever it pleases for itself, quite apart from God's guidance and direction. This is just what happened when the Israelites demanded a king to rule them instead of God and God said to the prophet Samuel: *"for they have not rejected you, but they have rejected Me, that I should not reign over them." (1 Sam. 8:7).*

They rejected the life of submission which the children of God live in obedience and submission to His will. Saul, the king whom they took for themselves, also followed his own desires and asserted his independence from God. He did not want God to order things for him, or direct his affairs, but began to administer everything according to his own personal ideas, without asking what God's will would be!

Sinners cut themselves off from God's will and also dissociate themselves from His guidance and direction. God has expressed this separation with His words, "They have rejected me and forsaken me ". He said, *"They have forsaken*

Me, the fountain of living waters, And hewn themselves cisterns; broken cisterns that can hold no water." (Jer. 2:13).

Quite simply then, sin is the state of being cut off from God, of having abandoned Him and rejected Him. The sinner feels no love towards God, nor any special intimacy with Him. **He has cut himself off from God, not only in his behaviour and manner, but in his heart, in his love and in his feelings too.**

His heart has begun to love other things which have taken the place of God. His concern is no longer for God, because he has started to be concerned about other things apart from God. These are what occupy his thoughts now and take up his time and divert his heart!

In the state of sin, the heart is cut off from God, in proportion to the extent that it loves the present world. If ones love for the world is total, then its separation from God will be total too, because *"friendship with the world is enmity with God " (James 4:4)* and *"If anyone loves the world, the love of the Father is not in him." (1 John 2:15).*

It is quite impossible for anyone to reconcile the two opposites, love of God and love of sin. He has to choose: either one or the other.

If you live with God, you will automatically be separated from sin and if you live in sin, you will consequently be separated from God. This means that you will be cut off from Him, from His kingdom, His will, His commandments, His love, His work and from fellowship with Him. As the Apostle says: *"God is light and in Him is no darkness at all. If we say that we have fellowship with Him, and walk in darkness, we lie and do not practice the truth." (1 John 1:5-6).*

God is light; sin is darkness. The Bible says: " *what communion has light with darkness?" (2 Cor. 6:14).* Whoever lives in darkness is obviously cut off from the light, meaning, from God. It was said about those people who cut themselves off from the Lord Jesus and rejected him, that they *"loved darkness rather than light, because their deeds were evil." (John 3:19).*

Therefore, when you live in sin, you are rejecting fellowship with God. What is this fellowship?

The spiritual life is fellowship with the Holy Spirit, as we hear it said in the blessing at the end of every service *(2 Cor. 13:14)* and through this partnership *we "may be partakers of the divine nature " (2 Pet. 1:4).* This does not mean that we become partners in the actual divine substance or divinity. Rather we become partners in activity.

The Spirit of God participates with us in our lives, working in us, working with us and working through us. If you are in sin, how can the Spirit of God have fellowship with you?

Have you broken this fellowship and cut yourself off from the work of the Spirit, by saying to the Lord: "You have your way and I have mine?"

By breaking away from the Spirit of God like this, you are going against the warning which the Apostle gave, *"Do notquench the Spirit." (1 Thess. 5:19). "Do not grieve the Holy Spirit of God, by whom you were sealed for the day of redemption.." (Eph. 4:30).*

The sinner is not only cutting himself off from partnership with the Spirit, but what is more serious is that he is resisting the Spirit, as St. Stephen said in his rebuke to the people. *(Acts 7:51).*

Sin is to be separated from the Holy Spirit and from the Son too, for the Son is *"the wisdom of God." (1 Cor. 1:21).* Therefore, one can reckon that anyone who is clearly foolish, must be cut off from the Son, otherwise his behaviour would be more prudent.

The Bible gives us an example of this in the parable of the foolish virgins *(Matt. 25:2).* The type of behaviour that comes from sinners is foolish behaviour, because it is unconnected to the divine wisdom of God. It is 'the foolishness of your people' of which we speak to the Lord during the Mass. Thus it was said in the book of Ecclesiastes, *"the fool walks in darkness." (Eccl. 2:14).*

Sin, therefore, is being separated from God, the very substance of wisdom.

Christ said to us, *"you in Me, and I in you " (John 14:20).* How can He be in us while we are committing sin?! How can we be in Him at the same time as we are in sin?! It is obvious that if there is sin in us, then, at that time, we are in a state of being cut off from Christ.

While we are in sin, how can we be a temple for the Holy Spirit?! How can the Spirit of God dwell in us *(1 Cor. 3:16)* while we are committing sin, for the temple of God is sacred? *(1 Cor. 3:17).*

There is no doubt then, that sin is a state of being separated from God and from His fellowship.

It is to be separated from that holiness without which no one will see the Lord, for only the pure in heart will see God *(Matt. 5:8).* Whoever loses the purity of his heart through sin, will not set eyes on God. In fact he will be isolated from Him.

Thus throughout history, sin has stood as a barrier between God and Man.

That intervening barrier came to be represented in the Old Testament in the Tent of Meeting.

This barrier, or curtain, which separated the people from the holiest of holies, so that they could not enter into the sanctuary, *(Ex. 26:33)* is a symbol for their separation from God through sin. This was the barrier which Christ destroyed by his crucifixion and which we, with our sins every day, try to build up again!

The Bible says about the foolish virgins, that "the door was closed" and the foolish girls stood outside. Between them and the Lord was this divide, the closed door. Though they begged, "Lord, Lord, open the door for us!", he did not open it for them. In fact he said to them *"I do not know you". (Matt. 25:11).*

They cut themselves completely from Him and from His kingdom and His throne and also from the other wiser virgins.

We read of the same kind of separation, in the story of the rich man and Lazarus.

While Lazarus was in the arms of his father Abraham, the rich man looked on 'from afar". Our forefather Abraham said to him, *"Between us and you there is a great gulf fixed". (Luke 16:26).*

In the life to come, the righteous will be in the heavenly Jerusalem, the place where God dwells with His people. No one unclean can enter here, nor anyone who is defiled, but only those whose names are written in the Book of Life *(Rev. 21:27).* It is here that the righteous will be separated from the sinners for ever.

God will divide the righteous from the sinners, the wheat from the chaff and the sheep from the goats and the wicked will be thrown into the outer darkness.

The darkness here means being cut off from the light, which is God and from the shining city of the heavenly Jerusalem. And the term "outer", applied to the darkness, signifies that the sinners will be beyond the group of the righteous, triumphant martyrs and far away from the Saints, whose lives were so remote from sin and were separated while on earth.

Thus, the sinner will be cut off in the afterlife from all those whom he had loved in this world.

Here on earth everyone is together: saints and sinners. In heaven however they will be separated. If anyone on earth loves a righteous person, he will not be able to see him in heaven, unless he repents here on earth and becomes righteous like his friend. By doing this, he will become entitled to a place in heaven alongside the righteous man.

If he remains a sinner, however, his connection with his loved one will be broken forever, whether that loved one was his son, brother, father or friend. He must become like his righteous friend, in order to enjoy his companionship in the eternal life.

If the two who love each other are both sinners together, what would happen to them then? I can tell you that the suffering which each one would find in the hereafter would give him no opportunity to think of his friend and even if it did, the suffering of the other would be an additional torment to him. They would derive no comfort from their companionship.

The only solution, then, which unites those who love, in order that they can enjoy each other's close companionship, is for them to live in righteousness here on earth, which will entitle them to be joined together in heaven.

Thus we see that sin separates a person from God, from the Saints, from his loved ones and from the angels too.

The Bible says that *"The angel of the LORD encamps all around those who fear Him, and he delivers them." (Ps. 34:7).* If you are among those who fear the Lord, you will enjoy the companionship of the angels here in this world and in heaven too. As for sinners, though, they cut themselves off by their actions, from the hosts of angels, for the angels cannot bear to see the sinners' awful deeds. As they sin, they are also surrounded by devils, who encourage them further in whatever wrong they are doing.

Sin is not just being cut off from God, but also from His angels, His saints, His heaven and kingdom, both here on earth and in the life to come.

In the story of the prodigal son, it is obvious that the young man was separated from his father. He dissociated himself from his father. This was what he had sought and had actually brought about himself, by his going away to a distant country *(Luke 15:13).*

At the same time as he was cut off from his father, the son was cut off from his home, which is a symbol of the Church, the house of God and he was cut off from the members of his family who symbolise the community of believers.

The same thing happened to the lost sheep: he parted from the shepherd and from the fold and the rest of the sheep ... and the story of the lost coin also tells of the same kind of situation *(Luke 15).*

Sin is a state of separation from God, which means that it is a separation from the very nature of righteousness and goodness. It means to be cut off from the divine plan which God laid down for your salvation and to be cut off from the divine course which God wishes you to take. This all comes as a result of being separated from the Truth and following what is false; for the Truth is God. *(John 14:6).*

The separation from God began from the first sin, that of Adam's.

Adam cut himself off from God's love and from that close companionship and fond intimacy which had existed between them. He began to fear God and to hide from His face and if he heard his voice, he would flee in order not to meet Him, because he could not bear to face Him. How could he face Him?!

There is another aspect to Adam's sin, which is that he became cut off from the Tree of Life, from the Garden of Eden and the place of meeting with God *(Gen. 3:22-23).* And what else? He was cut off from that divine image in which he had been formed. After sinning, he was no longer in the form or likeness of God.

The result of Adam's sin was that he was separated from God and being separated from God was itself a sin. But how did it all come about?

God used to order things for Adam in the Garden of Eden and drew up for him the plan that he was to follow. Adam, in his sin, began to go his own way, independently of God and began to decide for himself what he thought was good and the kind of future he desired when he and Eve would become *"like God, knowing good and evil". (Gen. 3:5)*

The first human being began to choose friends and advisers for himself, to whom he listened more than to God and he began to behave as if he were an independent person, determining his own life, with no need for God. That is how he disobeyed God's command and became cut off from Him, through the actual sin he committed.

Cain, when he sinned, was also separated from God. He became a restless wanderer on the earth, fearful and afraid, because in his separation from God he became cut off, not only from righteousness, but also from the help and safety which God had provided. Accordingly he requested from the Lord, (full of bitterness and grief), *"Surely You have driven me out this day from the face of the ground; I shall be hidden from Your face." (Gen. 4:14).*

Perhaps it was the same fear which the Prophet David had felt when he said, *"Do not cast me away from your presence and do not take your Holy Spirit from me." (Ps. 51:11).*

The phrase *"How long will you hide Your face from me?" (Ps. 13:1)* describes a situation which is much easier for a person to bear than to be banished from God's sight, as happened to Cain.

Saul's punishment was even harder, for *"the Spirit of the LORD departed from Saul ", (1 Sam. 16:14)* and it was said that directly afterwards "an evil spirit from the Lord tormented him." The moment Saul was cut off from God, he became under the domination of the devils. He became like an unfortified city, like a house without protection, an easy prey for the devils.

How difficult it is when you are caught up in that regression away from God!

It starts with disobedience against God and leads to contending with Him and being separated from Him. God's face becomes hidden to the individual and the Spirit of the Lord departs from him. He is cast out from God's face and evil spirits descend upon him to torment him.

But there is a condition still worse than being cut off from God, which is, to be *"thrown into the fire and they are burned" (John 15:6 and Matt. 13:42),* as was said about the branch which does not bear fruit. This is truly a very painful end for a branch which had once been part of the vine, but which now finds itself cut off from it and from the other branches.

From this example, then, we see that sin is also separation from the Church.

✤ ✤ ✤

Sin Is Being Cut Off From
The Community Of Saints

The Church is the community of saints who live in obedience to God. In the Creed we say, "we believe, in one Holy, Catholic and Apostolic Church." Even the church, as a building, is a place that is sacred to the Lord. In the Psalms we say, *"Holiness adorns Your house" (Ps. 93:5).* God says to his people, *"your camp shall be holy" (Dent. 23:14).*

Therefore the sinner, because of his sin or because he has turned his back on God and the Church, is cutting himself off, through his behaviour, or his way of thinking, from the holy community of believers. But it, too, dissociates itself from him.

It is only the actions of the sinner which set him apart from the believers. His life bears no resemblance to theirs, his principles differ from theirs, his behaviour and form, his ways and methods, all these set him apart from them, spiritually, mentally and in the direction of his life. In fact even his speech and expressions differ from the language used by the saints, just as it says in the Bible: *"your speech betrays you ". (Matt. 26:73).*

The Apostle John speaks about this separation when he says, *"In this the children of God and the children of the devil are manifest." (1 John 3:10).*

It is a separation of different types, according to their behaviour and the extent of their love for God. It is a clear distinction between the qualities of the sheep and those of the goats.

The Church is supposed to be united in thought, belief and spirit. Whoever detaches himself from this position, is expressing his personal wish to dissociate himself from this one spirit. By doing this, he becomes a danger to the holy community, which in turn cuts him off from its membership, after he has made it clear through his own action that he has withdrawn himself. The Bible says in such a case, *"put away from yourselves the evil person."* *(1 Cor. 5:13).*

This process of detaching itself, which the Church undertakes, is in order to retain the sanctity of its membership. Concerning those who have turned away from the faith, the Apostle John, who spoke about love more than all the other apostles, says , *"If anyone comes to you and does not bring this doctrine, do not receive him into your house nor greet him." (2 John 1-10).*

The sacred assemblies at the time of the Old Testament also used to separate off those who diverted from the faith and the principle of being *"shut out of the camp" (Num. 12:15),* as it was known in the Old Testament, was applied to those individuals.

This is how the process of separation takes place, so that whatever is characterised by sin and whatever is unclean, takes place outside the camp. Like what happened to Miriam, the sister of Moses and Aaron, whom God struck down with leprosy as a punishment, because she spread lies against Moses. *" So Miriam was shut out of the camp seven days." (Nu. 12:15)*

Owing to this, the sacrifices which were offered to atone for the people's sins and by the blood of which they were enabled to enter into the sanctuary, were burned outside the camp, so that the camp remained holy. *"For the bodies of those animals, whose blood is brought into the sanctuary by the high priest for sin, are burned outside the camp " (Heb. 13:11).*

In the Old Testament, the peoples of the world were parted from the holy people because of their sins. The Ark, too, was an example of this division.

Noah, his sons and their wives, who were in the Ark, represented those who obtained salvation and who became directly under God's guidance.

The unbelieving sinners, however, were left outside, under the rule of death, for the waters to sweep away, thus destroying them and destroying their sins with them. They had refused to enter, with Noah, into life, since their acts were unlike his. They had separated themselves from God who had created them for life.

Saint John the Beloved said of such people: ***"They went out from us, but they were not of us; for if they had been of us, they would have continued"*** *(1 John 2:19)* They had cut themselves off from us and no longer belonged to us.

The phrase *"they were not of us"*, is like the phrase of our Lord, *"I never knew you". (Matt. 7:23).*

Look at Judas: although he was one of the twelve, the phrase, "they did not really belong to us", which John spoke, could well have applied to him. He was one of our number and in the eyes of the people he was one of us too, but he was not one of us from the point of view of his heart and intentions. Thus he had not really been worthy to sit at the Last Supper with the other disciples. Therefore, when he took the morsel of bread, Satan entered him. The Bible says that as soon as Judas had taken the bread, he went out; *"Having received the piece of bread, he then went out immediately"(John 13:30)* and by going out, he isolated himself from the disciples forever.

Paul's disciple, Demas, went the same way as Judas.

He had started off as one of us, one of the senior preachers, one of Saint Paul's assistants. The Saint mentions him in his letter to the Colossians next to the name of Saint Luke the Physician *(Col. 4:14)* and he mentions him in his letter to Philemon, along with Mark and Aristarchus and puts his name before that of Luke *(Philem. 1:24).* It appears that he did not truly belong to us because, by loving the present world, he dissociated himself from the apostles, which is why Saint Paul says, in his final word on the tragedy of this man. *"Demas has forsaken me, having loved this present world " (2 Tim. 4:10).*

Demas dissociated himself from Saint Paul. His love for the world divided him from the entire ministry. His name was mentioned no more in the Bible, nor was he mentioned again as being among the community of believers. History records that he came to a painful end. He had not been able to bear the cross of Christ in the ministry and so had cut himself off from the life in Christ.

Sin is often a separation from the Cross of Christ.

It is to be cut off from the narrow gate by which the Lord ordered us to enter *(Matt. 7:13)*. It is also to be separated from the hardships about which the Apostle told us, when he said, *"We must through many tribulations enter the kingdom of God."(Acts 14:22).*

Sin is love of the world and the wide gate and the broad road. None of which accords with the Cross of Christ, about which Saint Paul said: *" I have been crucified with Christ; it is no longer I who live, but Christ lives in me ". (Gal. 2:20).* Whoever dissociates himself from the cross, dissociates himself from God and the community of believers.

How easy it is for a person who has allowed himself to sin and who has become used to sinning, to be cut off from the Church. He separates himself from the company of saints and seeks another group, whose members will agree with his behaviour and not reprimand him for his sins.

He also dissociates himself from the Church, the spiritual meetings, the Communion and confession. He plans a new course for himself in which he can engage in his sinful ways without being criticised or censured by anyone. What is more is that he also deprives himself of the benefits to be gained from reading the Bible and spiritual books, because he is unable to carry out the spiritual practices which they instruct.

It is not the Church which has cut itself off from him, but he who has detached himself from the Church. He has withdrawn from within, from inside his heart and feelings, in his way of thinking and in the direction of his life which he has taken. He has come to love, instead, the cravings of the body, or the lust of his eyes, or boasting of what he has or does *(1 John 2:16)*. Or he has come to love wealth, like the rich young man who withdrew from Christ and went away sadly, because he was very rich and was not prepared to give up his wealth to follow Jesus. *(Matt. 19:22)*.

The Serious Consequences Of Being Cut Off From God And The Possibility Of Returning To Him

As for you, my friend, do not let the Devil cut you off from God, or lead you away from Him step by step, until he has cut you off altogether and has cut all the spiritual ties which connected you to the Lord's love.

Wake up quickly and spare a thought for your salvation. **You can be sure that by being cut off from God, it is you who will be the loser,** for you will lose your purity of heart, your good standing and your eternal life. You will lose the true life, which is one of delight in the Lord and you will lose your soul, since you will lose your blessed eternity and the companionship of the saints. In return for that you will gain nothing here, as the Lord Jesus said: *"For what profit is it to a man if he gains the whole world, and loses his own soul?" (Matt. 16:26).*

What will you gain by cutting yourself off from God, His angels and His saints? You will just be making your fate the outer darkness in the lake of fire and brimstone. *(Rev. 20:10)* And you will be given the divine sentence against which there is no appeal.

But there is still an opportunity before you now to return to God.

It is unlikely that you will able to continue to be separated from God in this way. In your heart is a rebellious voice calling out to you to be reconciled to God. And God Himself wants you to return. For your separation from Him is not your proper position, nor is it the divine purpose of your creation.

I feel sure that you are bound to return.

You will find no peace in this troublesome world and so will turn back to God. Perhaps that lovely phrase which was used about the dove in the story of the Flood, could be applied to you, that when it found no place to set its feet, it returned once again to the Ark. *(Gen. 8:9).*

The Ark is the ship of rescue to which God is calling you and it is the place where you will be safe from the storms of this world. **Do not wait until you are sent some kind of hardship which brings you back, but come back by yourself, out of love for God, love for the good, or love for the eternal kingdom.**

I realise that sin has set you apart from all that is good and has given you nothing in return, you have lost God in return for nothing. The Apostle Paul called all the desires of the world worthless and said that for the sake of the Lord, "I have lost all things. I consider them rubbish, that I may gain Christ and be found in him, " and in fact he went on to say, *"Yet indeed I also count all things loss for the excellence of the knowledge of Christ Jesus my Lord" (Phil. 3:8).*

Do your best to put an end to this separation. **if you cannot, then cry out to God and say to Him: "O Lord, I can't bear to be parted from you for one moment longer, not even for a split second."**

You are life itself to me. Christ is life for me. If I am parted from you, I shall be lost and have no purpose. My life will have no meaning. It will be as if I am dead or do not exist. My real existence is in you. I cannot bear to be cut off from you, but if I should become separated from you for a while, be absolutely sure that it is only a temporary situation, something abnormal and something which I do not want.

So take me back to you, Lord, by any means. Restore my soul, because without you I cannot live. In you I live and move and have my being. *(Acts 17:28).*

If I am separated from you, I am cut off from power and grace and I am reduced to nothing. I will return to dust as I was, or rather become like the chaff which is scattered by the wind. *(Ps. 1:4)*

Dear Lord, do not let me be parted from you. Take me back, guide me along the paths of righteousness for your Name's sake. *(Ps. 23).*

Glory be to you, now and forevermore. Amen.

✛ ✛ ✛

✦

CHAPTER 2

THE RETURN TO GOD

"Turn to Me with all your heart, " (Joel 2:12)
"Return to Me and I will return to you," (Mal. 3:7)
"Repent, therefore and be converted, that your sins may be blotted out, " (Acts 3:19)

The Story Of Man's
Separatiopn From God

The relationship between man and God began very happily. It was one based entirely on love. It was God who began this relationship, by creating man and infusing him with the breath of life. He made him in His own image and likeness and placed him in the Garden of Eden, where He gave him authority over all the creatures.

God formed a relationship with man and would appear to him from time to time and speak with him. Man was God's friend: he enjoyed meeting Him in the Garden and learning directly from Him. God was man's spiritual guide in everything. He was the one who gave him the first instruction, with the first commandment.

So how did the sin occur? How was it carried out? What did it consist of?

Sin, in short, is separating oneself from God. It is when a person breaks away from God and renounces Him, so that he can do what he pleases. The result of this separation gave rise to all other problems and all other sins.

So, how did this separation come about then? How did it develop and what were its consequences?

1. Man was cut off from companionship with God:

When man became cut off from an intimate relationship with God, he began to form a relationship with another intelligent being. Unfortunately, though, that new relationship was with an enemy of God, with the Devil, that ancient serpent!

2. He became cut off from God in knowledge:

After having acquired his knowledge only from God, man began to acquire it in another way; from the advice and deceptions of the snake. He also expected to learn from the Tree of knowledge, which God had forbidden him to do. Thus he fell into a further separation.

3. He became cut off from God's command and His holy word.

4. He became cut off from God through the lusts of his heart;

He began to desire the Tree and to crave for its fruit and he found it, *"good for food, that it was pleasant to the eyes..."* *(Gen. 3:6)* This was how man fell into the desire for gratifying his instincts and for material things. The reason behind his desire to eat from the Tree in the first place, was a desire to become like God, as the serpent had tempted him. *(Gen. 3:5).*

5. Through being cut off from God, man was separated from the Truth:

Since God is Truth, if a person is cut off from Him, he is automatically cut off from the Truth and follows what is false. It is well known that the Truth is constant and never changes, but that which is not the Truth is very changeable. When a person is parted from the Right, he enters into the Wrong and thus enters into a perpetual state of change. Each day brings him a new stance and a new feeling and he becomes a changeable creature, unstable in his outlook.

6. By being cut off from God, man became cut off from Life: for God is Truth and Life. *(John 14:6).*

If a person is cut off from the real life, which is to be firmly established in God and have a stable faith in Him, he becomes dead from the spiritual point of view, according to what was said about the prodigal son by his father, *"for this my son was dead...." (Luke 15:24).* And the Lord's words, *"you have a name that you are alive, but you are dead.."(Rev. 3:1)* will begin to apply to such a person.

7. By being cut off from God, man became cut off from power.

The source of his power had been God. But by being separated from God, he became cut off from power and became weak.

The Devil overcame him and even the beasts gained power over him, as did his fellow men. Likewise, his own personality began to dominate him and he became a weak creature who could not stand upright or fend for himself.

8. Through being cut off from God, man forfeited his authority:

He became cut off from the authority which he had been given by God over the other living creatures. He no longer had the same authority over the beasts of the earth.

9. He also forfeited his dignity and respectability:

The respectability which he had enjoyed, through being in the image and likeness of God, departed from him and he lost this divine image with his fall into sin. As a result of losing his respectability, he was expelled from the Garden of Eden and stood before God like a guilty offender who deserved punishment.

When the Devil saw man banished from God's presence, guilty of sin and punished, he found it an opportunity to dominate him and so the Devil set himself up as the lord of this world. That is how his title became *"the ruler of this world". (John 14:30).*

10. As a result of his separation from God, man began to collapse and fear entered him:

He began to be afraid of God, instead of loving Him and enjoying an intimate relationship with Him.

Then he began to be afraid of his fellow men, like when Cain was afraid and said, *"anyone finds me will kill me". (Gen. 4:14).* Man also began to fear the animals and anxiety, confusion and worry came over him.

11. With his separation from God, man became separated from the life of the Spirit.

Thus he came to be dominated by material concerns and by the body. He fell into the sins of the flesh. The sins of the flesh began to attack even the prophets and men of God, such as Samson, David, Solomon and others. It was said: *"For she has cast down many wounded, And all who were slain by her were strong men.." (Prov. 7:26).*

12. Through being cut off from God, man went deeper and deeper into sin:

Little by little his sins began to grow and step by step man began to fall further, until he had gone to extremes in doing what was evil and squalid and in devising cunning tricks and arts and until his sins outnumbered the hairs on his head.

This, then, is the history of sin on the earth and man's separation from God. It is a history that records man's tragedy and from which we learn that sin never relaxes its efforts until it is brought to completion.

When the Devil makes someone fall into sin, he is not content simply with that, but continues to get the person more and more involved until he is unable to resist any longer. Then the Devil destroys him.

What is the solution then?

The only solution is to return to God and form a relationship with Him.

If sin is dissociating oneself from God, then the only cure is to dissociate oneself from sin and return to God. There is no other remedy besides this.

Separate yourself from sin, with all your heart, not only because it will wear you out, or because you are afraid of the Judgment Day and punishment, but because this sin of yours will take you far away from God and will cut you off from His sweet companionship.

What Does It Mean
To Return To God?

In short, it means... forming a real and sincere relationship with God in your heart.

When I say a relationship, I do not just mean the external signs and practices of religion. Some people imagine that to return to God means that all they have to do is follow a programme of prayer, fasting, spiritual exercises, spiritual readings, meetings and mataniyas (prostrations).

All these are, fine, but do they spring from a heartfelt relationship with God, or not? In all these devotions, is there a love for God or not?

Without this relationship of the heart and without this love, you will not really have come back to God, however much you pray, fast, read and perform mataniyas.

It is only through a relationship with God, which is one of love, that these spiritual means take on their effectiveness and strength. So the feeling must come from the heart first of all and then these practices will naturally follow. This is why the Lord says in the book of the

Prophet Joel, *"Turn to Me with all your heart". (Joel 2:12).*

God says, *"Turn to Me with all your heart, With fasting, with weeping, and with mournin rend your heart and not your garments. Return to the LORD your God". (Joel 2:12-13).*

It is the return of the heart, therefore, which is required: the heart first of all. And it is from this returning heart, which is crushed in remorse before God, that fasting and tears of repentance gain their strength.

It is amazing how many people get caught up in the means to reach God, such as the devotions, the spiritual exercises and the disciplines, but forget the end to which they are directed, which is God!

For example, there is the type of person who has set his heart on reciting a group of psalms, who becomes disheartened when he fails to reach his target, but who becomes happy if he manages to complete them, regardless of whether he has had any connection with God during this recital!! No, this is not the way.

The Psalms have a tremendous spiritual force, they have blessings and effectiveness and a profound influence of their own, provided that they come from a heart that is in a relationship with God.

Without this relationship and without the feelings of the heart, even though you pray, your prayer will be marked by apathy and by a confusion and wandering of your thoughts.

If you pray without any feelings, without enthusiasm or faith and without feeling God's presence, then the whole thing turns into just an empty exercise, without the relationship within the heart giving this practice any weight or value.

A person might fast, for example, but he might not bring God into his fast.

All he is interested in is the period of abstinence and in seeing how long he can continue it and in his abstention from food and his asceticism. Perhaps he has set himself not to eat anything sweet, or anything cooked, or perhaps he has decided to restrict himself to bread, water and salt. If he manages what he has set himself to do, then he feels pleased with himself and feels that he has been successful in his fast. As far as the idea of using fasting as a means of bringing him closer to God is concerned, this idea has probably never occurred to him!

The heart is the fundamental element and it is by the heart that we can distinguish between two types: One person might pray the Psalms and cast out devils by them, while another might pray the same Psalms and it is as though he is not praying at all, since he does not have any relationship with God in his heart. Needless to say the prayers of the second type produce little effect.

One person might fast and obtain mercies and forgiveness from God, as did the people of Ninevah. Yet someone else might fast and not receive such blessings, because he has not admitted God into his fast, like the Pharisee.

The heart, then, is the deciding rule. We want the return to God to be with the heart.

The return to God also means a firm and lasting return. It should be one in which there is no backsliding, for some people imagine that they have returned to God, yet live unbalanced lives, swinging from one thing to another. They might spend one day with God, full of enthusiasm for Him, while the next day they are caught up with the desires and lusts of the world. What was said in the story of the Ark, about the raven which Noah released after the Flood, that it *" which kept going to and fro" (Gen. 8:7)*, could well be applied to these people.

Do not let your return to God be just a return for the sake of special occasions, or for the fasts, or for the sake of following certain instructions from your spiritual father, or because you want something in particular, because this would make it a return of convenience. After the particular reason for your return to God had passed, you would simply go back to your previous sinful ways and once again be separated from God!

You can learn a lesson about returning to God, from the stories of the saints.

Take St. Moses the black for example. When he returned to God, he returned with all his heart and never went back to his earlier sins. In fact he kept on growing and growing in his spiritual life until he became a spiritual guide and example to many.

There was also Mary the Copt, Pelagia and Augustine and others, all of whom returned to God, never again to part from Him. Moreover, they all went on to progress continually in their spiritual growth, from a life of repentance, to a life of holiness.

To return to God means to return with a new heart.

God Himself says concerning this: *"I will give you a new heart and put a new spirit within you" (Ezek. 36:26)* St. Paul says: *"be transformed by the renewing of your mind", (Rom. 12:2)* which means adopting a new way of thinking and weighing things up, according to a new scale of values, rather than the old one. When St. Paul began to value the importance of thinking about spiritual matters, sin lost any influence over him.

Let the return to God be with fasting and self-abasement, just as the people of Nineveh returned to Him.

They heard the Prophet Jonah's warning that after forty days the city would be overturned *(Jon. 3:4),* but they did not lose hope of God's mercies and they returned to Him with fasting and humility. So what did they do?

"They declared a fast and all of them, from the greatest to the least, put on sackcloth. When the news reached the king of Nineveh, *"he arose from his throne and laid aside his robe, covered himself with sackcloth and sat in ashes.". (Jon. 3:5-6)*

Thus all the people covered themselves with sackcloth and cried out vehemently to God and returned from their wicked ways. Thus God returned to them.

In the book of Joel, we see the same fasting and self-abasement, when the Prophet said, *"..Consecrate a fast, Call a sacred assembly; Gather the people, Sanctify the congregation, Assemble the elders, Gather the children and nursing babes; Let the bridegroom go out from his chamber, And the bride from her dressing room. Let the priests, who minister to the LORD, Weep between the porch and the altar." (Joel 2:15-17).*

We see the same situation in the fast of the Prophet Daniel and his humbling of himself before the Lord. He said: *"Then I set my face toward the Lord God to make request by prayer and supplications, with fasting, sackcloth, and ashes. And I prayed to the LORD my God, and made confession." (Da. 9:3-4)* and *"I, Daniel, was mourning three full weeks. I ate no pleasant food, no meat or wine came into my mouth, nor did I anoint myself at all, till three whole weeks were fulfilled." (Da. 10:2-3).*

In the individual, the return to God is distinguished by an eagerness, a careful and painstaking attitude and a serious approach.

Whoever returns to God is very joyful about his return and is enthusiastic for this reconciliation which has taken place between them. He is also very careful so as not to let any backsliding or relapse occur to make him fall back to what he was.

He has experienced before, the problems that come from being too easy going and tolerant about sin. He has learned how if he is careless about his way of thinking, it soon changes into a feeling in his heart and then into a desire which flares up within him. This is how sin begins to dominate him and it becomes difficult to escape from it.

He therefore examins every thought and feeling carefully.

He is careful about those sins which seem little in significance, as about those which are significant. His attitude is like that found in the Song of Songs, when it says: *"Catch us the foxes, The little foxes that spoil the vines ". (Song 2:15)* & to the sin itself, at its outset, he says: *"Happy the one who takes and dashes Your little ones against the rock " (Ps. 137:9).* By doing this he is being faithful in little things...

By such careful examination as this, you can test your faithfulness in returning to God. For if you are easygoing about sin and not strict with yourself, you are not being sincere in your return to God. Your heart is weak inside and will be easily brought down.

The true return to God is one of strength. It is a return in which God will give you a strength which you will feel in all aspects of your spiritual life: the strength to overcome sin, a strength to grow spiritually and to rise up. As mentioned in the book of the Prophet Isaiah, *"He gives power to the weak, And* *to those who have no might He increases strength. Even the youths shall faint and be weary... those who wait on the LORD Shall renew their strength; They shall mount up with wings like eagles, They shall run and not be weary, They shall walk and not faint".(Is. 40:29-31).*

Samson, the strong man, lost his strength when he sinned, because the grace of God departed from him. But when he returned to God, his strength came back to him.

Ask the Lord, then, to give you strength to return and to give you a strength that will stay with you as you return to Him, strength from His Holy Spirit... a strength which you can feel in everything which your hand touches, so that you will be just like the righteous man mentioned in the first Psalm, *"Whatever he does shall prospers." (Ps. 1:3).*

Take for example a person who was very ill but who, after a blood transfusion, found that his strength and vitality returned quickly as the new blood entered him. In just the same way, the penitent returning to God, will feel his strength and vitality flowing back to him, through the action of the Holy Spirit entering him.

Whenever you find yourself feeling weak, look up and say to the Lord with absolute sincerity: **"Why do I feel so weak? Has your grace left me because I have sinned?'** *"Restore us, O LORD God of hosts; Cause Your face to shine, And we shall be saved!"* (Ps. 80:19) What a beautiful Psalm this is which the Church sings to God, addressing Him in humility: *"Return, we beseech You, O God of hosts; Look down from* *heaven and see, And visit this vine..... which Your right hand has planted" (Ps. 80:14-15).*

Will God return and watch over this vine? Does God want us to return to Him?

God Wants Us To Return

God calls us in love, *"Return to Me and I will return to you."* *(Mal. 3:7)*; This phrase carries a great deal of emotional significance:

1. God is reminding us that our true and original state is with Him and that sin is something foreign that enters us from outside.

It is as if He is saying to us, Your separation from me is not your true and original state. Your true position is to be firmly rooted in me, to abide in me, because I am the vine and you are the branches. *(John 15:5)* and in nature the branch is always firmly attached to the vine. " I am the head and you are the body, you are the limbs." *(Eph. 5:23).* So for you to be firmly established in me is something natural.

I am not calling you, then, to come to me, but to return to me.

Return to the natural position which has been yours since the beginning. Return to the divine form which was yours on the day that you were created. This separation of yours is something that has happened accidentally, just a temporary situation. It is not right for you to remain in this state.

The life of righteousness and holiness is not something new to you, but is your original nature in which my relationship with you began and in which you will live with me in eternity."

2. The words "Return to me" bear proof of God's loving kindness:

What were we but dust and ashes, before God called us to return to Him?! It is God's love, which is inexpressible, which reminds us in the hymn "O my beloved come back to me", that God wants our relationship with Him to be close and permanent. He, whose name is Immanuel, meaning *'God with us' (Matt. 1:23)* takes delight in the sons of man. It is He who says to us, *"I will come again and receive you to Myself; that where I am, there you may be also.." (John 14:3)* It is He who has made the heavenly Jerusalem, the dwelling of God is with men and he will live with them. They will be his people and God himself will be with them and be their God. *(Rev. 21:3).*

3. It is good if you take the initiative, in your return to God:

For He is always the one who begins everything and He is the one who asks and He is the one who calls us to Him. What is more, He sent the prophets to us for this purpose and laid down for us the mystery of repentance.He promised us that if we return, He will forget the past entirely and never mention it again. *(Jer. 31:34).*

What does it mean, though, when He says, "Return to me and I will return to you "? Does it mean that our return must come before His, or that it is a condition of His return?! No, far from it! All He means by this is to say:

4. My return to you is guaranteed. The important thing is your return.

At any time that you call me, you will find me with you. In fact I am standing knocking at the door of your heart, that you might open it to me *(Rev. 3:20)*. But the difficulty comes from your side. "If anyone hears my voice and opens the door, I will come in and eat with him and he with me." That is why I say, "I will return to you", meaning, open the door of your heart that is shut against me, then "I will return to you". By this, God means 'I shall enter those hearts of yours, from which you have cast me out, by rejecting me in your sinfulness'.

'Come back to me, for I am with you, even though you do not feel my presence'.

St. Augustine was certainly right when he said, "You, O Lord, were with me, but I was not with you". God is with us and acts on our behalf, even when we are deep in sin. He is searching for us even though we have strayed from His fold and He calls us, 'Come back to me'.

What does it mean, then, that He will return to us, if we return to Him?

His return to us means that we will feel that He is present with us. God's 'return' does not mean that He was away from us and is then going to come back. All that is necessary is for us to become aware once again that He is with us. If this feeling comes back to us, we will feel that God has returned to us.

Sometimes we imagine that God has left us, while it is **we** who have left Him. This reminds me of a time (in 1957) when I was so moved by the departure of the sun at the time of sunset and aware of how wrong we are to think that the sun is **leaving** us for the night, that I wrote in my journal: "I said to myself at sunset: it is not that the sun has hidden its face from the earth, but rather that the earth has turned its back on the sun".

Yes, the truth is that the sun is fixed! It is The earth that revolves. What we call the 'sunset' is just an expression for the revolving of the earth around the sun.

This is analogous to the relationship between us and God. We feel that He has vanished and left us just because we have turned our backs and are no longer facing Him.

If we return to God, we feel that He is with us and we feel His light shining upon us, because God is the same for ever He does not move around or change *"whom there is no variation or shadow of turning". (James 1:17).*

Look, for what has taken you away from God.

Ask yourself at what point on the road did you part from Him? What sin divided you from Him and His love? know for sure   that this separation has come from you.

"Remember therefore from where you have fallen ! Repent... "
(Rev. 2:5).

Your feeling that God is far away from you is a feeling that the intimacy which had existed between you no longer exists, as a result of the fading of your love for Him, or because your sin has taken you away from Him.

5. The phrase "Return to me" also carries another emotive meaning, which is: God wants us to follow Him with all our hearts and will and love, which is why He says, "Return to me".

It is as if He is saying, "I cannot force you to love me, nor would I put pressure on you to form a relationship with me. The matter depends on your free will. If you want me to return to you, I shall return to you. And if you do not, then you are free to follow your own path."

However, a person might say: "I want to but I am weak...,"

In this case, it is enough that you wish to return, God will do the rest for you. As one of the Saints put it, "Virtue simply wants you to desire what is virtuous and nothing more than that..."

Throughout history, it is God who has begun the relationship with mankind.

It was He who began the relationship with our forefather Noah, by choosing him saving him and setting him apart from evil and the wicked. It was He who began the relationship with our forefather Abraham, whom He also chose and set apart from evil and the wicked similarly with Moses and his people. It was God who began the relationship with the twelve disciples when He said to them: *"You did not choose Me, but I chose you and appointed you... " (John 15:16).*

Trust in God's desire for you to return to Him. At the same time, know that it is essential that you cooperate with Him in the desire and the action. You must believe absolutely that you need God in your life and that without Him you can do nothing. *(John 15:5)*

You must come to understand, from deep within, how sweet it is to live hand in hand with God and how sublime and beautiful it is to lead the spiritual life and to return to the image of God, to that purity and innocence which Adam once had.

You must recall the vows which you made to God at your baptism, when you promised to fight the Devil and all his evil deeds, all his wickedness and stratagems.

That was the time when you made a lovely new beginning, when you were born again of God and clothed in Christ. *(Gal. 3:27)* It was when you shed the old person in order to live a new life *(Rom. 6:4-6)* and when you became cleansed of every sin.

Little by little you forgot your vows and forgot that you were a son of God. You abandoned your purity and dissociated yourself from God and now you want to return to Him.

In order to return to God, remember that you belong to Him.

You do not belong to yourself and are not free to behave as you please. You belong to God who created you and who redeemed you. St. Paul says to us: *"Or do you not know that your body is the temple of the Holy Spirit who is in you, whom you have from God, and you are not your own? For you were bought at a price; therefore glorify God in your body and in your spirit, which are God's." (1 Cor. 6:19-20).*

The Devil has wrested you away from God. But God, out of his love for you, is holding you fast, because you belong to Him and He is saying. *"Return to Me".*

"Return to your purity, which you had before when you were abiding in me. Return to your calm and peace, for you will have none without me."

All those who go far away from God, or who are separated from Him, find no peace for themselves and live wearisome and troubled lives. St. Augustine experienced this and said to the Lord, "Our hearts will always be restless, until they find their rest in you."

The Lord, who wants us to return, says to us, when we are caught up in the troubles and anxieties of the world, *"Come to Me, all you who labor and are heavy laden, and I will give you rest ". (Matt. 11:28).*

If you return to God, all your problems will be solved. You will live without a problem, because the only real problem in your life is to be separated from God. All other problems are a result of this. So if you return to God, you will live in peace: in peace with God and peace with yourself and with peace in your heart. "This is what the Sovereign Lord... says:

"In returning and rest you shall be saved; In quietness and confidence shall be your strength." (Isa. 30:15).

Therefore, return to the Lord. Return to the light, so as not to walk in darkness. Return to the Spirit, so as not to live for material things, or according to the flesh. Return to life, for sin is death.

In this way your youth will be renewed like the eagle's.
(Ps. 103:5) You will feel comfort in your spiritual life and enthusiasm will flow back into you as you go about your daily affairs. Your life will become interesting and will take on a purpose. You will feel that God is within you and that He is with you. You will experience His kingdom and learn the sweetness of living closely with Him. You will know the meaning of the phrase, *"it is good for me to draw near to God".* *(Ps. 73:28).*

God wants us to return to Him. He wants us to have salvation and wishes us to love Him as He loves us. That is why He says: *"Turn to Me, with all your heart". (Joel 2:12)* And the Divine Inspiration records this beautiful phrase for us, *"Do I have any pleasure at all that the wicked should die?"*

says the Lord GOD, "and not that he should turn from his ways and live?" (Eze. 18:23).

God wants us to return to Him so that we might live... which is because sin is a state of spiritual death on earth and its consequence is eternal death.

God wants us to return, then, for our own good.

In addition to this, there is His loving kindness, for He does not delight at the death of a sinner. The death of a sinner is something which saddens God's heart, without any doubt. When a sinner returns to Him, *"there will be more joy in heaven over one sinner who repents than over ninety-nine just persons who need no repentance." (Luke 15:7).*

The Apostles rejoiced and told the good news about the return of the Gentiles, to their disciples. *(Acts 19:3).*

The Bible uses the term 'return' in connection with the Gentiles, because faith in God was man's original condition, which applied to all people, long before the Gentiles separated themselves from this faith and from God. When they believed, this was considered return to God. *(Acts 15:19).*

An important fact which you must understand, my friend, is that God wants you to return to Him, more than you want it!

A sinful person may not care about his personal salvation and may not think of returning to God. Or he may enjoy sinning and prefer to continue to sin, feeling that a return to God would deprive him of all his pleasures.

In all this, God is striving continuously to bring back such a sinner to Him, by every means.

There are many great stories which show how God strives after sinners.

In chapter 15 of the Gospel according to our teacher Luke, the story of the lost sheep and the lost coin are mentioned. St. John's Gospel mentions how Christ strove to bring back the Samaritan woman at a time when she had no idea at all that she would encounter Him.

There is also the way that God stands at the door knocking, asking the soul to open and let Him in. I'm likely to get carried away telling you all these examples... The important thing to note is that all the missions of the Prophets have concentrated on this subject, which is God's desire that we should return to Him and not just this desire of His, but also the action which He takes to achieve it.

At this point, we might ask: 'If our return to God is something pleasing to Him and God desires it and strives for it and we too desire it... how then do we return to Him?' Are you wondering: How do I return to God?

The most effective means to help you return to God is prayer.

✠ ✠ ✠

Prayer Is The Means Of Returning

Pour out your heart before God and say to Him: 'O Lord, I want you. I want to come back to you. Please rescue me from my state and draw me back to you once again.

Without you I am nothing. When I lost you, I lost my life. I lost my happiness and delight. My life became without any meaning or interest. I want to come back to you, O Lord, but *"those who trouble me rejoice when I am moved " (Ps. 13:5). " Many are they who say of me, "There is no help for him in God.""*. *(Ps. 3:2).*

I lost my strength when I went far away from you. Give me some of your strength. Please give me the divine assistance to help me to return to you.

Cast yourself before the Lord and wrestle with Him and say to Him: **'I shall not get up from here unless I have received your special blessing and feel that you have taken me back and count me among your children. I do not just want you to forgive my sin, I want you to remove from my heart any love of sin, once and for all**. I cannot come back to you, if there is any love of sin in my heart. What should I do? Should I wait till the desire to sin has gone from my heart and then return to You? Yet it is only by You that I can be saved from it!

So I come to you with my sin, just as I am. You are the one who can take it from me.

If it were within my power to abandon the love of sin, I would have returned to you long ago. Save me from it, so that you can lead me in the procession of your victory.

Take any desire to sin from my heart and remove any domination which sin might have over my will. *"Purge me with hyssop, and I shall be clean; Wash me, and I shall be whiter than snow". (Ps. 51:7).*

Just as you have given me the instruction to return, O Lord, give me the strength to carry it out.

Believe me, my friends, the person whose prayers are successful is the person whose repentance is sincere.

St. Isaac The Syrian was right when he said, "Anyone who imagines that there is another way to repentance besides prayer, is deceived by the devils". Thus by prayer, you gain the strength with which to return to God. So force yourself to pray, rather than to engage in any other spiritual activity. In your prayers, wrestle with God, struggle with Him and talk to Him, even when you are still in the state of sin from which you wish to be saved.

Be determined in your prayers, that you will get from God the strength to return to Him.

Some people imagine that when they pray they are **giving** ... giving God words, time and feelings. But at its deepest, prayer is a process of **taking**, during which you feel that you have gained from God spiritual delight, blessing, strength, help and holiness in life. In fact, just for you to have made a connection with Him during your time of prayer, is enough to bring this into effect.

God is ready to listen to your prayer and to give, but the problem is this: that **many people, in their prayers, do not wait until they have received..!**

For example, someone might say a few words in prayer, become bored quickly, or fed up with praying any longer and so he leaves it without having gained anything..! God looks upon such a person and wonders, how he could have gone off so quickly without waiting to receive even a promise or some comfort.

So hold fast to God, and say to Him, "I shall not leave you... I shall not let you go, until I feel that you have accepted me and taken me back into your love."

Prayer requires patience. It requires a struggle with God, in which you must prove that you are serious in what you ask. You must show that you are serious in your prayer of repentance and in your request for help to return to Him, so that when God answers your prayer and gives you strength, you will use it well and not waste it.

Talk to God in a very personal way in your prayers and ask Him: Do the weak fail to reach your kingdom, O Lord? Here I am, see how weak I am and how incapable of getting there with my human strength! Hold my hand and do not leave me to my weakness. Cleanse me and purify me, as you have cleansed and purified others. Didn't you say, *"Ask and it will be given to you"? (Matt. 7:7)* Here I am asking and didn't you say, ".. my Father will give you whatever you ask in my name.. "? here I am making my request.

O Lord, I shall hold on to all your promises and ask you for them. At least I shall hold on to your words. *"I will give you a new heart and put a new spirit within you; I will take the heart of stone out of your flesh and give you a heart of flesh. "I will put My Spirit within you and cause you to walk in My statutes, and you will keep My judgments and do them". (Eze. 36:26-7).*

Dear Lord, in my case, where are these promises?

Here I am standing here, holding on to the horns of the alter. I am not one of those who pray for a couple of minutes and then leave. I take my stand and wait here for You, O Lord. I shall not abandon my prayer until I can leave it, feeling that I have had your grace bestowed on me for my repentance and until you have taken me back to you.

Nevertheless, dear Lord, please forgive my boldness, for I am only a child of yours and have just gone astray. Please treat me as a young son who knows nothing, while You, as a compassionate father know how to give your children good gifts. *(Matt. 7:11).*

Keep striving with God, as you would with a close loved one, with persistence, with humility, with perseverance, with tears and by talking to him and by whatever means you can, until you receive.

Trust that by such a struggle, you will receive comfort and enthusiasm, from your prayers or during your prayers and that you will feel that your state of separation from God is over once and for all. You will feel, too, that you have not just been repeating empty words in vain, like the unbelievers, but that you have been pouring out your whole soul before God, as did Hannah, the mother of Samuel.

Hannah prayed very hard and wept very bitterly and made very strong vows and did not leave the temple until she had received a promise that the Lord would give her the desire of her heart. *(1 Sa. 1:15-17).*

Let it be the same for you. Do not leave your prayers, unless you have formed a new relationship with God and have returned to Him.

After such prayer as this, it would be highly unlikely that you would abandon your praying and go off and sin against God! You would certainly feel ashamed of your prayers and of having told God, that you would never leave Him.

This is how prayer teaches repentance and leads the person back to God and to His love.

But perhaps you might say: "I don't feel like praying at all."

My advice to you, then, is to pray just as you are and say to God, "Forgive me, dear Lord, if I pray without enthusiasm, but I pray out of the emptiness which is in my heart. It is you who gives me enthusiasm and warmth. It is you who pours your heavenly fire into my heart. Accept my prayers as they are, with all their faults. Things never start off perfect, for perfection only comes from you.

I **am praying, even though it is without any spirit! I believe that you will give me of your Spirit.** I would be mistaken if I said to you, O Lord, that with my human strength and willpower I could change into a spiritual person. There is no way that I could do that, for it is only by Your strength, Your blessing and grace and by Your Holy Spirit, that I could ever take on the image which You want me to have. It is only through Your guidance alone, with You holding my hand, leading me step by step, as You would lead a little child who is just learning to walk, that it can happen."

This is how I want you to pray and to receive from the Lord. **Listen, during your prayer, for the voice of God, speaking in your heart.** As David said in his Psalm, *"I will hear what God the LORD will speak, For He will speak peace To His*

people and to His saints; But let them not turn back to folly"
(Ps. 85:8).

David began the Psalm with a request, then after feeling God's response, he ended the Psalm in thanks. He said: " *O LORD, do not rebuke me in Your anger, Nor chasten me in Your hot displeasure* " And at the end of the Psalm he says: " *Depart from me, all you workers of iniquity; For the LORD has heard the voice of my weeping. The LORD has heard my supplication; The LORD will receive my prayer* " *(Ps. 6: 1&8-9).*

This is the sort of prayer which indicates that you feel that the barrier which has been between you and God has disappeared. You feel as if the angels are climbing the steps to heaven with your prayers and bringing back down to you what you have requested. *(Ge. 28:12).*

You feel as if God's hand is stretching out to wipe every tear from your eyes and as if the prayer of the Prophet David, in his great Psalm, is being brought into a reality within you. " *Let my supplication come before you". (Ps. 119:170).* You feel, as if one of the twenty four priests has taken your prayer and placed it in a golden brazier and raised it as purifying incense to the throne of God. *(Rev. 5:8).*

You feel as if one of the Seraphim has taken a burning coal from the altar and touched your lips with it and has said to you: *"Your iniquity is taken away, And your sin purged "*. *(Is. 6:7).*

Truly, I say to you, by such prayers you can return to God. Let us cry aloud to Him, saying: *" Restore us, O God of our salvation," (Ps. 85:4)* and "Restore

our fortunes, O Lord, like streams in the South*." Then our mouth was filled with laughter, And our tongue with singing ...* " and we will say, *The LORD has done great things for us, And we are glad '" (Ps. 126:2-4).*

Adversity As A Reason
For Returning To God

The troubles which afflict us are not all of one kind:

There are troubles that afflict a person which are like a cross that he must carry for the sake of God, in order to obtain his crown, as happened to the Apostles and men of faith. *(Heb. 11:36-7).*

Other difficulties are there to test our faith, or to teach us to pray, *(James 5: 13)* or that we might have the opportunity to be examples of patience, as happened to Job. *(Job 5: 11).* There are other adversities which are designed to make a person aware of his weakness and to teach him to be humble, as happened to St. Paul *(2 Cor. 12:7).* There are yet other problems which come upon us because our sins have cut us off from God's grace. It is this last kind which I would like to tell you about now.

These adversities which come as a result of our withdrawing from God's blessing, will not disappear byway of human wisdom, or through the use of human strength. There is only one means of solving them and that is by following God's words to us:

+ *"Return to Me and I will return to you." (Mal. 3:7).*

If a person returns to God with prayers and fasting and by humbling himself and if he returns to Him with sincere repentance, then he will once again have an awareness of God in his life. God's grace will return to him as it had been before and will no longer be withheld from him. Consequently, the person's problem will also come to an end, as the factors causing it will have disappeared.

In the book of Judges, there are great many examples which illustrate this clearly.

The Bible says: *"Then the children of Israel did evil in the sight of the LORD, and served the Baals; and they forsook the LORD God of their fathers, who had brought them out of the land of Egypt; and they followed other gods from among the gods of the people who were all around them, and they bowed down to them; and they provoked the LORD to anger. They forsook the LORD and served Baal and the Ashtoreths. And the anger of the LORD was hot against Israel. So He delivered them into the hands of plunderers who despoiled them; and He sold them into the hands of their enemies all around, so that they could no longer stand before their enemies." (Jg 2:11-14)* **The Israelites were unable to stand, since the hand of the Lord was no longer with them.**

When the hand of the Lord had been with them, the Red Sea had parted for them and drowned Pharaoh and his troops. The rock had split open to give them water and they had beaten Og, king of Bashan *(Josh. 12:4)* and Sihon, king of the Amorites *(Josh. 13:21)* and all the nations on the earth.

On this occasion, however they had been delivered into the hands of their enemies and had been unable to withstand them. The word of the Lord stood before them: "Return to me and I will return to you". When they cried aloud to the Lord, He heard their weeping and saved them.

How extensive is the Lord's love, even at a time when His blessing has been withheld! For the Bible says that He came back and "saved them out of the hands of their enemies ... for the Lord had compassion on them as they groaned under those who oppressed and afflicted them. *(Judg. 2:18).*

In all your troubles, do not say: "What should I do with my enemies, who have triumphed over me?" But rather ask yourself: "Is the hand of God with me or not? Have I left God and has His blessing left me, though it was with me before?" Listen to God's words, *"Return to Me and I will return to you"* and then, quickly return to the Lord and you will find that the divine aid, returns to you, making you, as it did to Jeremiah, " A fortified city and an iron pillar, And bronze walls..... They will fight against you, But they shall not prevail against you. For I am with you," says the LORD, *"to deliver you." . (Jer. 1:18-19).*

The story is repeated in the book of Judges... The people sinned and did evil and worshipped Baal and the Lord sold them into the hands of Cushan, king of Aram *(Judg. 3:8).* Then they cried aloud to the Lord and he raised up a deliverer for them, named Othniel and he rescued them.

The Spirit of the Lord was upon Othniel and the Lord gave Cushan into his hands, *"So the land had rest for forty years".* *(Judg. 3:11).*

On every occasion that they faced a dire adversity, they returned to God and He returned and saved them. Then they went back to their sins and to worshipping idols and so their troubles returned. This made them cry aloud to the Lord and He came back to them and rescued them.

As we go through history, we hear about the captivity in Babylon and Ashur. This also happened because the Israelites had done wrong and had worshipped idols. We read in the Bible of how the children of God wept by the rivers of Babylon and hung their harps on the poplar trees. *(Ps. 137).*

Yet all the while they were captives, the phrase "Return to me and I will return to you" echoed in their ears. During their captivity, there appeared holy men, such as the prophet Daniel and the three young men who were in the fiery furnace and the Prophet Ezekiel and various men of faith, such as Nehemiah, Ezra and Zerubabel, showed them examples of holy zeal. Then the Lord returned from the heat of His anger and restored His captive people.

How did the Lord return to them?

He returned because of the tears of Nehemiah and Ezra.

When Nehemiah heard that the walls of Jerusalem had fallen and that its gates had been burned by fire, his heart blazed with anger and he said: " *I sat down and wept, and mourned for many days; I was fasting and praying ..... then I said .. "O Lord... I confess the sins of the children of Israel which we have sinned against You. Both my father's house and I have sinned. "We have acted very corruptly against You....O Lord let Your ear be attentive to the prayer of Your servant......"* (Neh. 1:3-11).

And so the Lord returned. He bestowed His blessing upon Nehemiah before the eyes of the King of Persia and Nehemiah was able to rebuild the walls of Jerusalem.

Then there was Ezra, who wept for the sins of his people and rent his clothes.

At the time of the presentation of the evening sacrifice, Ezra rose up from his self-abasement and knelt down in his torn garments. He stretched out his arms to God and said: *"O my God, I am too ashamed and humiliated to lift up my face to You, my God; for our iniquities have risen higher than our heads, and our guilt has grown up to the heavens....... You our God have punished us less than our iniquities deserve, and have given us such deliverance as this, "should we again break Your commandments...? "O LORD ... You are righteous! , for we are left as a remnant." (Ezra 9:3-15).*

Ezra fasted and his people fasted with him. *(Ezra 8:21)* He wept and he made the people weep bitterly with him. *(Ezra 10:1)* The Lord heard and returned to His people.

With his fasting and prayers and weeping, Ezra was able to bring all his people back to God and God returned to them. In the previous stories, the sinfulness of the entire people had angered God and so His blessing had been withdrawn from them, yet the prayers and crying of one person were able to bring God back to His people.

In other cases, it may have been that the sin of just one person was the cause of the whole trouble, like the sin of Achan, son of Carmi *(Josh. 7)* and like the fleeing of the Prophet Jonah from God *(Jon. 1)*.

Thus return to God, not just for your own sake, but for the sake of those around you too. **In every trouble that surrounds you and them, consider how you can return to God.**

Do not think about those people around you who are causing you trouble, but think of yourself and of your relationship with God and of your return to Him. And have faith that the harshest and most powerful of enemies will not be able to maintain their stand when a pure eye, flooded with tears, is raised up to God, or when a pure heart speaks with God, or when innocent hands are stretched out to Him.

Our relationships with other people are only superficial, secondary relationships.

The most important thing is our relationship with God. As for our relationships with other people, these are only a consequence of our relationship with God... they change as our relationship with Him changes.

When the Sabeans took the cattle and the donkeys of the righteous Job and the Chaldeans took his camels, *(Job 1: 14-17)* he did not complain or blame God that they had taken them, he just said, *"The LORD gave and the LORD has taken away" (Job 1:21).* Return to God and He will restore everything to you.

If you return to God, evil and the wicked will have no power over you.

Not only your enemies who rejoice that you have fallen, will not have any power over you, but even the Devils will not be able to overcome you; however much they might surround you, like bees round a honeycomb, they will die out as quickly as burning thorns. *(Ps. 118).* As the Prophet David says: *" Many a time they have afflicted me from my youth; Yet they have not prevailed against me." (Ps. 129:2).*

Niether sin nor lust would be able to overcome you, because the Lord is with you. He will give you strength and help and will lead you in triumphal procession in Christ *(2 Cor. 2:14).* If His heavenly grace leaves you, then the least thought will be able to overcome you and will weaken your resistance.

Then you will hear the voice of the Lord in your ear: "Return to me and I will return to you". Raise your heart to God and return to Him, that your strength might come back.

What does the phrase, "I will return to you" mean?

It means, "I will return to you with all my strength and help and I shall return to you with all my love: and we will be as we were before. It will be as if your sins had never been." *For I will forgive their iniquity, and their sin I will remember no more."* *(Jer. 31:34).* In short, "I will return to you" means, "we shall be reconciled".

Let us now go on to talk about reconciliation and being at peace with God.

✥

CHAPTER 3

RECONCILIATION WITH GOD

" we are ambassadors for Christ, as though God were pleading through us: we implore you on Christ's behalf, be reconciled to God" (2 Cor. 5:20)..

Sin Is Contending Against God

It is wrong to put yourself on the opposite side to God.

A sinful person is one who opposes God, who defies Him and breaks His commandments. He abandons God's will in order to carry out his own wishes, making himself independent of God and dissociating himself from God. He loves sin more than he loves God, however much he might claim, with his tongue, to love Him!

The sinner flees from God. He does not like to talk with Him. And if he stands in prayer, then the Lord's words, *"This people honour Me with their lips, but their heart is far from Me,"* *(Mark. 7:6)* apply to him. Thus his prayers are without love, without emotion and without any spirit and are probably only said for the sake of performing a duty, or to satisfy himself. The sinner does not talk much about God and does not feel any loving intimacy with Him. The sinner also feels estranged from God, because sin has created a barrier separating him from God.

Sin may develop from this level of contending against God, to the level of actually fighting against Him. St.

James the Apostle talking about this said: *"friendship with the world is enmity with God". (James. 4:4)* and St. John the

Evangelist says: *"If anyone loves the world, the love of the Father is not in him." (1 John 2: 15).*

Since sin is a kind of rift between man and God, we begin our masses with the prayer of reconciliation. Before we raise the Ebrosfarin (large linen covering the oblations) to pray the mass of the Saints, we pray the prayer of peace and reconciliation, because we must reconcile the people with God first of all, before we can pray and before we can offer the divine mysteries.

Thus we address God, the Son, in the Gregorian Mass saying, "You interceded for us with the Father and You broke down the barrier separating us and destroyed the old enmity between us. You reconciled those living on earth with those in heaven."

The worst aspect of sin is that it is directed against God Himself: David, the Prophet, knew this fact well, which is why he said to the Lord, in his psalm of repentance, *"Against You, You only, have I sinned, And done this evil in Your sight ". (Ps. 51:4).*

David had obviously wronged Uriah the Hittite and Bathsheba, Uriah's wife, just as he had wronged himself, by spoiling his chastity, his purity and his morality. Nevertheless, none of this was of chief concern to him, when he said to the Lord, "Against you, you only have I sinned". That is because David could see that his sin was fundamentally against God, against His commandments and against His love and as a consequence of that, it was against others too.

The righteous Joseph also realised that sin was first and foremost an offence against God, during the scene with Potiphar's wife, when he said: **"How then can I..... and do such a wicked thing and sin against God?"** He did not say, "and sin against Potiphar, or against Potiphar's wife", he simply said, "*and sin against God". (Gen. 39:9)*. This is because sin is disobedience against God and opposition to Him. It shows a lack of love for God and shows that He has been banished from the individual's heart. It is a rebellion against God and a scorning of His commandments.

It was for all these reasons that Adam became afraid, after his downfall and hid from God's sight, for he knew that he had angered God by sinning.

It is a sad fact that whenever we sin, we grieve the Holy Spirit of God. *(Eph. 4:30)* The first consequence of sin is that it upsets God, the second is that it destroys the person. To atone for the result of the first, burnt sacrifices were offered *(Lev. 1)*. To atone for the result of the second, sin offerings were presented *(Lev. 4)*.

The Lord Jesus came to serve as the act of atonement for both of these sacrifices: so that he would appease the heart of the angry father, like a burnt sacrifice and so that he would save mankind, who was doomed, by being an offering for his sin.

Probably what causes most pain of all to a person's heart, is not only the realisation that he has sinned against God, but rather that he has created a rift between himself and God and that God is no longer pleased with him.

The sacrifice of a burnt offering, in the Old Testament, was to appease God, to satisfy His angry heart. Thus the first sacrifices were made under the Mosaic law. It is mentioned in the first chapter of the book of Leviticus. It said that "when the burnt offering was to be presented it had to be offered *"at the door of the tabernacle of meeting before the LORD" (Lev. 1:3),*.so that it would be acceptable to the Lord." Three times in the same chapter it is spoken of as, *"a sweet aroma to the Lord." (Lev. 1:9, 13 & 17)*.

Its purpose was confined to this one point, which was to please God and fulfil His justice. Its purpose was not to save man, because that was the intention behind the sacrifice of sin. For this reason, no one partook of it, as they did of the sacrifices given for sin. It was consumed entirely by the fire, until it turned into ashes. *(Lev. 5:8 & 13)*. The fire represented divine justice.

It is as if the person presenting the burnt offering is saying to the Lord, as it is being offered: **"What concerns me now is not my salvation, but that you should be pleased."**

"What am I but dust and ashes?! I am the person least worthy to offer sacrifices on my behalf. Whether I am saved or not, is not my chief concern, but what is most important of all, O Lord, is that your heart should approve of me. After this do with me as you wish. I have sinned against you and I want to be reconciled with you. After I have become reconciled to you, will come my request for forgiveness and I know that you will forgive, without my need to ask."

What you should feel is the kind of feeling felt by a son, whose only concern is that his father should be pleased with him. It is not the feeling of the slave, whose only concern is to be saved from punishment.

Are you as keen as this to please your heavenly father and be reconciled to Him? Do you strive to heal the rift between yourself and God? Or do you do like Adam, who fled and hid himself from God?! Do you say as the righteous Job said, *"Is there any mediator between us, Who may lay his hand on us both," (Job 9:33)?* Do you feel that sin has put you far away from God and created a breach between you?

There is something else which I need to tell you about, which is that:

Sin Being Unfaithful To God

In general, sin is disloyalty to God and a betrayal of Him. The sinful person is unfaithful to the love of our compassionate God, who loved us and showed us the full extent of his love. *(John 13:1)* and showered us with His good gifts.

Since God has considered us to be His children and has become a father to us, when we sin against Him, we are really letting Him down as a father. When we sin, we are also being unfaithful to the promises which we made to God at our baptism and which we have made on those occasions when He has saved us and which we have made whenever we have taken the Communion.

We are being unfaithful to God, because we, His children and chosen ones, join forces with His enemies, the Devils and we deny Him in preference to gratifying our own desires.

God asks us to be faithful, saying to each one of us, *"Be faithful until death, and I will give you the crown of life." (Rev. 2:10).* But we, by sinning, betray this fidelity. Our hearts do no abide in God's love, but are shaken by every whim and by every desire. They do not possess that steadfast, faithful love.

If we sin against God, we are really doing something worse than His enemies are doing, for their attacks are only considered to be hostility towards Him. Their enmity does not contain that element of betrayal which is involved in our sins, because of our position as sons of God, called after His name. How can we attack Him like this and join forces with His enemies? How can we sell our souls, which He bought with His blood and how can we banish His Holy Spirit from our hearts? Is not all this considered to be the utmost disloyalty?

Perhaps those who did not know God before have an excuse. But those who have known Him and lived with Him and experienced Him and upon whom He has bestowed His holy mysteries, who have then gone on to reject Him, how can they not be seen as traitors to His intimacy and love?!

God Himself called this desertion of Him, being unfaithful, when He said, *"For the house of Israel and the house of Judah Have dealt very treacherously with Me". (Jer. 5:11).*

The theft committed by Achan the son of Carmi was considered a betrayal of the Lord. *(Josh. 7:1).* And marrying foreign women was also considered an act of unfaithfulness. *(Ezra 10:2).*

The Bible says, that king Saul, ".. *died for his unfaithfulness which he had committed against the LORD, because he did not keep the word of the LORD, and also because he consulted a medium for guidance " (1 Chr. 10:13).*

The negligence of the priests and the Levites in the service of the house of the Lord, was considered unfaithfulness, which is why the good king Hezekiah said, " our fathers have trespassed and done evil in the eyes of the LORD our God; they have forsaken Him, have turned their faces away from the dwelling place of the LORD... and put out the lamps. and have not burned incense or offered burnt offerings ... " *(2 Chr. 29:6-7).*

As long as sin continues to be contention against God and unfaithfulness towards Him, then there must be reconciliation with Him.

The heart must return to Him and confess its betrayal. It must feel remorse and humble itself before Him, in order to be forgiven and so that a new relationship from a faithful heart can begin.

The intention is that the reconciliation be enduring and irreversible. Because if you are reconciled with someone and behave as if you were his friend, but then come back the next day and upset him and insult him, this is not a real reconciliation. Reconciliation is the return of love, a true and lasting love.

The history of sin ends in reconciliation with God. **The amazing thing, however, is that it is God, whom we have rejected, who strives for this reconciliation by every available means.**

✢✢✢

God Is Reconciled With Us

What was the work of all the prophets and apostles whom God sent to the world, except to establish peace between God and man? Look at St. Paul, who says: *" we are ambassadors for Christ, as though God were pleading through us: we implore you on Christ's behalf. Be reconciled to God." (2 Cor. 5:20).*

It is the Lord Jesus, then, who sends these ambassadors to us, asking us to be reconciled to Him. What a wonderful love this is!

It can be quite difficult for you if you decide to go to a person to make it up. You keep wondering whether he will accept your overtures of peace or not. Here it is God who wants reconciliation and who asks for it and who sends messengers for that very purpose, through whom He works with His grace and Holy Spirit. He says to mankind, *"Come now, and let us reason together". (Isa. 1:18).*

Not only this, but God even strives to be reconciled with those who are disobedient and stubborn, for He continues: *"All day long I have stretched out My hands To a disobedient and contrary people." (Rom. 10:21).*

Imagine God stretching out His hand all day long to befriend these stubborn people. The *"all day long"* means that He is doing it with all His patience and with hopeful expectation. He does not get tired of striving to reconcile sinners. It is He who looks at your heart and says: *"This is My resting place forever, Here I will dwell, for I have desired it." (Ps. 132:14).*

It is He who says to your soul, which is so precious to Him, *" Listen, O daughter, Consider and incline your ear; Forget your own people also, and your father's house The King will greatly desire your beauty " (Ps. 45:10-11).*

In actual fact, the reconciliation of the Lord with man, was the reason for the divine incarnation.

Saint James AI-Sarugi said, "There was a rift between God and man and since mankind was unable to restore peace and be reconciled to God, God came down to man, in order to be reconciled to him."

The reconciliation of man with God, is also the aim of the redemption.

The blood of our Lord Jesus was the price of this reconciliation. The Apostle says concerning this: For God was pleased to have all his fullness dwell in him *".and by Him to reconcile all things to Himself, by Him, whether things on earth or things in heaven, having made peace through the blood of His cross." (Col. 1:20).*

See how dear the price of your reconciliation was and how precious your soul is to God. For we *" were reconciled to God through the death of His Son." (Rom. 5:10) "that God was in*

Christ reconciling the world to Himself, not imputing their trespasses to them." (2 Cor. 5:19).

What part did Christ take in this reconciliation? The Apostle says: *"For He Himself is our peace, who has made both one, and has broken down the middle wall of separation... through the cross, thereby putting to death the enmity.." (Eph. 2:14-16).*

Christ reconciled us to the Father by putting an end to the hostility and removing the barrier which divided us from Him.

But we still sin and need to be reconciled with God every day. This is why there is the "ministry of reconciliation" which is the work of the apostles and the various orders of priests.

St. Paul says concerning this, that God *"has given us the ministry of reconciliation"* and that he *"has committed to us the word of reconciliation".* *"We implore you on Christ's behalf.. Be reconciled to God" (2 Cor. 5:18, 19-20).*

All the pastoral work of the priests, preachers and teachers is this "ministry of reconciliation" in pursuit of peace between God and man and for the most part, this is also the work of the holy sacraments.

God wants to be reconciled to you by every possible means. He says to you: "This rift between us has gone on for long enough, let us begin a new relationship, however much you run away from me, even if you go to a distant country, or hide behind the trees, or take you heart far away from me, I shall still send messengers and prophets for the sake of your reconciliation. I shall send you ministers and shall send you my blessing. I shall provide the spiritual means and prepare the opportunities."

What else will God do?

God is also ready to send difficulties, either to us or to our loved ones, if need be, for the sake of our reconciliation. Perhaps a person will not come to God out of love, but will come after a blow of some sort, like Joseph's brothers, who were led to reconciliation through adversity. *(Gen. 44).*

The Lord says: *".. Call upon Me in the day of trouble; I will deliver you, and you shall glorify Me." (Ps. 50:15).* When adversities oppress you and you find that only God's tender loving heart shows you kindness, you will become reconciled with Him as you remember His love.

Every adversity whispers in your ear: Be reconciled with God.

Remember, too, that God reconciles you to Him, for your own sake. He also reconciles you to Him in order to restore you, to cleanse you, to purify you and to make you holy. His love for you is so great that He will not abandon you, in case you go astray, or the enemy of Goodness, the Devil, preys upon you.

God is afraid that you will perish if you go far away from Him and that you will change your principles and ideals and become like the other people in the world, worldly, materialistic and concerned with physical things. Thus He seeks reconciliation with you in order to save your soul. It would be a great pity if you were to lose this opportunity to be reconciled with God.

Great are the benefits that you will gain from this reconciliation.

In making peace with God, you will find forgiveness and salvation. The Lord will wash you so that you become whiter than snow. *(Ps. 51)*. He will wipe away your sin and not remind you of your previous sins. *(Jer. 31:34)*. In reconciliation you will gain inner peace and you will be reconciled to your own soul too. There will no longer be a struggle inside you.

Through reconciliation you will return to God's fold, you will no longer feel estranged from His house and His kingdom. In fact you will become one of those who dwells in the house of the Lord. *(Eph. 2:19)* Through reconciliation you will win eternal life, because according to the Lord: *"For what will it profit a man if he gains the whole world, and loses his own soul?" (Mark 8:36)*.

If on occasions you spend a great deal of effort to make it up with other people, with whom you have only a temporary relationship on earth, then it stands to reason that you should be much more concerned about being reconciled to God, with whom you can have an eternal relationship that will never end! Be sure that you realise, then, how important God is for you and how important it is for you to be reconciled to Him.

Just look at how much effort the Lord has spent for the reconciliation of man, who is really only dust and ashes. **But does man, this pile of dust and ashes, feel the same about being reconciled with his Creator?!** I fear that what the Lord said to Jerusalem and her people applies to us: *" How often I wanted to gather your children together, as a hen gathers her chicks under her wings, but you were not willing!". (Matt. 23:37)*.

The Lord is standing at the door, but we do not open it to Him. How can reconciliation take place? What are the obstacles that hinder some people from responding and what is the solution?

How Reconciliation Takes Place

The first condition, without which there can be no reconciliation, is:

1. That you have a sincere desire to be reconciled to God:

The aim of all the means of grace and spiritual influences and all the other things which are conveyed to us by our spiritual guides, is to implant this idea in your heart, whereby you say with sincerity, "O Lord, I want to be reconciled with you." If your desire is honest and comes from deep within your heart, then without doubt you will find the means to connect yourself to God. God Himself will unite you to Him.

2. By having the desire, you begin the process, providing you are serious in your desire:

There are some people who may say that they want to come back to the Lord, but they have a thousand voices in their hearts crying out, "I want to sin".

The desire for reconciliation with the Lord, comes only from their lips; it is not in their hearts. Someone might say "I want to be reconciled...", but deep down he does not really want it, because being reconciled to God will deprive him of many things which he loves and will cause him to enter by the narrow gate, which is against his wishes.

Perhaps the real reason behind all this is a favourite sin within his heart, or a habit which dominates him, or a fixed characteristic of his, or an intractable will.

Perhaps the thing that is hindering you from being reconciled with God, is that you are in the kind of state which our teacher, St. Paul, described in his Epistle to the Romans: *"for to will is present with me, but how to perform what is good I do not find.."(Rom. 7:18)* and *"For the good that I will to do, I do not do; but the evil I will not to do, that I practice. ..... it is no longer I who do it, but sin that dwells in me." (Ro. 7:19-20).*

If this is your problem, my friend, my advice to you is to:

3. Strive hard to follow God, so that He can change your heart:

Say to Him, "O Lord, save me from my heart and from my sin and from my natural inclinations. Let none of this be an obstacle in the way of my reconciliation with You. You have changed many peoples' hearts and probably their state were even worse than mine. I wish that I could be one of those whose hearts You changed. O Lord, you changed the hearts of Moses the black, Augustine and Mary the Copt and Arianus and others... Is it so difficult for You to change my state?"

Consider my situation to be a complicated one, but when placed before your boundless power, it will not be hard to solve.

O Lord, I am unable to restore my own heart and make it peaceful, which is the first thing that I need in order to be reconciled with you.

It is only **You** who can mend this heart of mine and put into it the holy feelings appropriate for this reconciliation.

My son, why don't you say to God, *"give me your heart"*. *(Prov. 23:26)* "take it as it is..."

Purge it with your hyssop and it will be clean. Wash it and it will become whiter than snow. *(Ps. 51:7)*. I am not asking you just to mend this heart of mine, but to create within me a pure heart *(Ps. 51)* and give me a new spirit. *(Ezek. 36:26)*. **If there is no love for you in my heart, then please give me this love.**

Do not blame me for my lack of love, but just pour out your love into my heart by the Holy Spirit, according to the words of your Apostle. *(Rom. 5:5)*.

Consider me as a little child, who wants something but does not know how to get it; who desires something but is unable to attain it and *"Direct my footsteps." (Ps.119)* for I stumble so often.

If I am not serious enough about the salvation of my soul, it is sufficient that you, O Lord, are serious about redeeming this soul of mine.

If my willpower is not strong enough to save my soul, then certainly Your grace will be strong enough to save it.

If I do not yet really want to live with You because of the blemishes in my character, then it will be enough that You want me to live with You. Your will can do whatever is necessary.

If You, O Lord, abandon me to my own will and to my weakness, then I shall perish. Consider me as someone who is ill, who is not strong enough to heal himself, or to go to the doctor. Say the word so that your servant will be healed. *(Matt. 8:8).*

Offer to the Lord a prayer from your heart, that if your effort is not strong enough, then your prayer can make up for the deficiency. For *"The effective, fervent prayer of a righteous man avails much." (James 5:16).*

In being reconciled to God, do not rely too much on your own understanding, or on your human strength. *"Trust in the LORD with all your heart, and lean not on your own understanding." (Prov. 3:5).* Just take from God the strength which will support your weakness.

What God wants from you is your heart and will and faith.

What is meant by 'will' is not some tremendous show of strength and determination, but rather the desire to be close to God. For a person might be weak, yet God can give him the strength to act. In fact God Himself might even work through him and work with him. As St. Paul said: *"for it is God who works in you both to will and to do for His good pleasure." (Phil. 2:13).*

God wants your desire for reconciliation, because He never forces anyone to be reconciled with Him.

If you can offer Him this desire, He will act together with you. I am not saying that He will do it all alone, otherwise this might encourage a person not to make any effort. On the other hand, your effort in working together with Him, will indicate the seriousness of your desire to be reconciled to Him.

So far, then, we have said that you must have a sincere desire for reconciliation and that when you are serious about your desire, you should try to carry it into effect by praying and asking for help to overcome any obstacles which you might encounter. What else do you need to do?

4. Avoid anything in the future which might upset God, so that your reconciliation does not suffer a relapse and you return to the state you were in before. If you are reconciled with God, don't then turn back and join forces with His enemies.

Endeavour to avoid all potential areas of sin, because very often the heart yearns for God, but then its desire grows cold, under the influence of some kind of opposition. People are easily influenced and you can see how easy it is for human nature to go from one extreme to another, if it has not yet become firmly and fully established in God.

Make sure that you realise, too, that to be reconciled with God does not just mean that all you have to do is to say the words 'I have sinned'. Many people have said this before but have not benefited from it, because their words were not sincere.

Reconciliation with God means to live a life that is distinctive by its being one that is pleasing to God. It means a productive way of behaviour in which the individual strives, in practical ways, to please God and win His love. It is not enough just to be confined to a negative approach, such is not entering into any new form of hostility towards God, or opposition to Him. **There has to be a positive orientation in which the reconciliation is turned into love.**

5. Therefore I advise you to live within the realm of divine influence:

Spend your time with God and occupy your thoughts with Him. Do not let your relationship with God be only for that one day a week which we call 'the Lord's day', but let it be for the whole week. Let it be a relationship which lasts a whole lifetime.

Do not imagine that reconciliation with God just means that you only ever do what is righteous. It is, of course, very good if you can behave virtuously, but always bear in mind that **virtues are not the goal but the goal is God Himself.**

Virtue, in the sense of doing good, is only a means in which you can express your closeness to God, but your real goal is to achieve this closeness with God, in continuous love.

If you follow a life of virtue and righteousness, do not be tempted to consider yourself more highly, or expect others to consider you someone special. But rather let it be that by this piety you become bound much closer to God, so that your heart becomes worthy to remain in His dwellings. So be very alert and careful!

Do not leave God's circle for your own personal one, or even for the one of virtuousness.

Let the center of your interest and the focus of all your efforts be God and His love. Let your heart always be aglow and keep your relationship with God always strong.

A mistake which many people make is to practice various virtues and doing good, but without having an awareness of God in their lives, or in their emotions. But as far as you are concerned, say to God: "I want to feel Your presence, O Lord and I want You to make Yourself known to me. I want to be alone with You and open my heart to You. I want to love You more than anyone else and more than anything else. I am prepared to lose everything for Your sake and I count it all worthless in comparison to finding rest in You and finding my existence in You. *(Phil. 3:8).*

This is the fervour that comes from reconciliation and which turns into love.

In this enthusiasm, hold fast to all spiritual means which kindle your emotions towards God and strengthen your relationship with Him.

6. Read about the Saints of Repentance who were reconciled with God and who loved Him.

Mediate on the lives of the Saints and how God filled their hearts and how eager they became to please Him. Their stories will kindle within you a love for God and resurrect a love for goodness hidden in your heart. For there exists deep within everyone, however much he falls into sin, a longing for goodness. For God created man in His own image and likeness and evil is something extraneous which intrudes into the human character.

Whenever a person does something bad, he hears a voice inside him protesting against it and there comes a time when he can no longer silence this voice.

When he reads the biographies of the Saints, or sees an example of true virtue, his heart will easily be stirred from within and he will feel his inferiority. His eyes will be filled with tears and he will acknowledge that spiritual excellence is truly the highest thing of all, whether he aspires to it and progresses towards it or not. Any person who is enslaved to a particular desire, must have inside him something which protests against it, however much he tries to ignore it.

7. In your reconciliation with God, do not feel any regret at those pleasures of the world which you have left for His sake. For these are wars from Satan.

Do not be like Lot's wife, who looked back as she was leaving Sodom. *(Gen. 19:26)* On the contrary, you should rather feel happy that you have been saved from this past. The sinner loses any sense of his own worth in his own eyes and in the eyes of others.

If Satan tempts us to sin now, he will condemn us with it on the Day of Judgment before God and other people and he will consider us to be among his troops because we were led by him. He will consider himself to possess any of our limbs or organs that have submitted to him. We can remain hopeful of success in our fight against the Devil, if we remember what our Lord said about him: *"for the ruler of this world is coming, and he has nothing in Me.." (John. 14:30).*

8. If you are reconciled with God, take care to continue your reconciliation. Give a considerable thought to the prospect of eternal life and the kingdom of God.

Let your thoughts be far-ranging and not confined only to those few days which we live on earth, with all their ties to material things and the body. If you have laboured for the Lord and have carried a cross in your reconciliation with Him, then say to yourself that: " *I consider that the sufferings of this present time are not worthy to be compared with the glory which shall be revealed in us".. (Rom. 8:18).*

Those who live in a good relationship with God live fixing their eyes *"not at the things which are seen, but at the things which are not seen. For the things which are seen are temporary, but the things which are not seen are eternal." (2 Cor. 4:18).*

9. **Be on your guard against new concepts which might upset your spiritual balance,**

Which say to you: What is wrong in doing this? or which play down the enormity of sins, or which call them by another name or offer justifications to excuse them all. Under such influences sin no longer appears to be wrong and the spiritual feeling disappears and the person does not feel that he is upsetting God in any way by what he does. He probably imagines that God is angry with him for no reason at all!

A person in this state, therefore, does not find any justification, or see any reason, for asking for reconciliation, since he does not feel that he has done wrong! One of the obvious and essential conditions or reconciliation, though, is for the individual to feel sorry for his sins. This can only come about if a person holds fast to the proper healthy spiritual values which the Saints have handed down to us through their examples and through their words and their lives.

10. Be quick to respond to the voice of God in your heart.

If you hear the voice of God inside you calling you to Him, do not ignore it, or be slow to respond, lest your heart should harden and you lose the spiritual effect. As the Apostle said: *"Today, if you will hear His voice, Do not harden your hearts as in the rebellion." (Heb. 3: 5).*

11. One of the basic conditions of reconciliation is that you must prefer God to yourself.

The most dangerous thing that hinders reconciliation is that you prefer what you want, to what God wants and that your self becomes an idol which you worship. For as long as you seek to please yourself in everything, you will not be able to be reconciled with God. It is good for us to bear in mind what our Lord Jesus said: *"Whoever desires to come after Me, let him deny himself, and take up his cross, and follow Me (Mark 8:34).* Even in the Lord's prayer which He taught us, He put our own personal requests at the end, while what pertains especially to God is at the beginning.

To deny yourself on earth, is to win yourself in heaven.

This is why the Lord said to us: *"For whoever desires to save his life will lose it, but whoever loses his life for My sake will find it." (Matt. 16:25).* And He also said, *" He who finds his life will lose it, and he who loses his life for My sake will find it" (Matt. 10: 39).*

What have you lost for the sake of the Lord? What lengths have you gone to for His sake?

If you truly wish to be reconciled to God, then remember this principle and keep it in your heart.

God first, others second and yourself last of all.

Be reconciled to God and reconciled with others and then you will be at peace with yourself and heaven and earth will be at one with you.

12. When you are reconciled with God, be prepared to feel a change in your life.

Do not carry on living in the same way, with the same character and behaviour and thoughts, but let your reconciliation with God change your life, for the better. That personality of yours which Satan used to dominate before, will become a character which possesses the strength to fight the devils and the humility to stand before God. It will show a spirit of love, service and tolerance in its dealing with others.

May the Lord be with you.

www.ingramcontent.com/pod-product-compliance
Lightning Source LLC
Chambersburg PA
CBHW071820020426
42331CB00007B/1559